TAJH AND THE DOLLAR HE KEPT

Artissa Shorter

ISBN 978-1-63885-030-4 (Paperback)
ISBN 978-1-63885-032-8 (Hardcover)
ISBN 978-1-63885-031-1 (Digital)

Covenant Books, Inc.
11661 Hwy 707
Murrells Inlet, SC 29576
www.covenantbooks.com

Stand on truth, stand on facts, but most importantly, stand on LOVE. May your soul forever be at peace. In loving memory of Ivy A'Lailaa Baker. Stand strong Laderrian Prince.🤍

Hi. I'm Tajh Ali, but you can call me Tajh.

I really like playing with my toys and playing with my friends. I also like to ask a lot of questions.

I have so many toys, and I am always asking for more.

My mom said I have to buy my next toy with my own money.

Whenever I do good in school and help around the house, Mom gives me money for my allowance.

My allowance is the reward I get for doing something well.

5

Today, Mom said my allowance will be ten $1 bills. That's a lot of money.

7

Imagine all the things I can buy!

Oh, I almost forgot. Mom said, before I can spend any money, I must first put some up.

In other words, she wants me to save some of my money.

How am I to know how much
I should save?

I always hear Mom talking about saving 10 percent or more of her money.

12

How am I to know what 10 percent is? I mean, hey! I'm only five years old!

Do you remember when I said I like to ask questions? Well, let's ask Mom, what does it mean to save 10 percent?

When speaking with Mom, she showed me an example using beans. Each time I counted nine beans, she would take the tenth bean and place it in a bowl.

So for every $10 I receive, I must save at least $1? Or this means I must save at least one $1 from the ten bills I have.

That's not much at all. I should have no problem saving $1.

Every time I receive an allowance or gift of $10, I will be sure to save at least $1.

Being that I am always helping out around the house, doing well in my studies, and on my best behavior, I'm sure my savings will add up in no time.

18

Now on to the
toy store I go!

Take a look at this awesome toy I purchased!

22

Mom said, once my bank is full, I'll be able to go to a big bank and have my very own account.

ABOUT THE AUTHOR

Artissa is a woman, a mother, and a friend. Each day, she strives to make the quality of her life and the lives she comes in contact with better. She is from the small town of Opelika, Alabama. She earned a degree from the University of Alabama at Birmingham. She is the mother of two children, Tajh Ali and Aijah Kamal. Artissa is very passionate about financial literacy and self-love. She enjoys learning and teaching others what she has learned and what she practices as it relates to finances and self-love.

CPSIA information can be obtained
at www.ICGtesting.com
Printed in the USA
LVHW070125050422
715319LV00005B/60